World War One

LIFE IN THE TRENCHES

Robert Hamilton

Trans
Atlantic
Press

A soldier could see
no more than ten yards

After entering France in 1914 the Germans immediately dug trenches to protect the land they had gained, forcing the Allies to follow suit. Much of the war on the western front was subsequently fought from these trenches, which rapidly became associated with the needless killing of young men as they were sent by their commanders 'over the top' to their death. Coupled with this were the appalling conditions they were forced to live in; with limited supplies and equipment, constant risk of disease and minimal local medical facilities.

The first trenches were fairly simple structures but they rapidly became deeper and more complex. Normally about 12 feet in depth, they were dug in a zigzag line which prevented artillery fire or bomb blasts from travelling very far, but also limited a soldier's line of vision to no more than about 10 yards. The earth bank facing the enemy, known as the parapet, had a fire step built into it to allow men to watch the enemy, and the rear section, the parados, helped protect soldiers from the shells falling behind them.

BELOW: Soldiers armed with pickaxes make their way to the front. In many cases their first challenge was to dig the trenches they were to live in for the next few weeks. According to British guidelines it was estimated 450 men would take 6 hours to build a 275-yard front-line trench system.

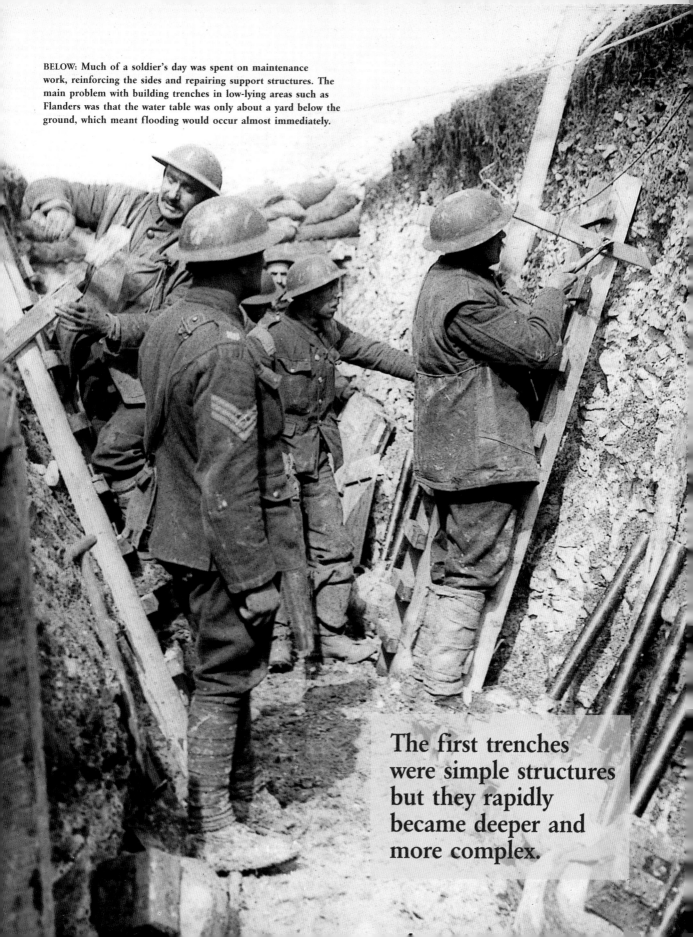

BELOW: Much of a soldier's day was spent on maintenance work, reinforcing the sides and repairing support structures. The main problem with building trenches in low-lying areas such as Flanders was that the water table was only about a yard below the ground, which meant flooding would occur almost immediately.

The first trenches were simple structures but they rapidly became deeper and more complex.

BELOW: Infantrymen from the British XIV Corps begin their advance during the Battle of Morval in September 1916. They successfully took the village and neighbouring Gueudecourt, rescuing them from German control.

A vast network of tunnels

The sides of the trenches were reinforced with wire mesh, wooden frames and sandbags. Wooden ducking lined the floor, although as the war progressed wooden frames raised it up to provide increased drainage. Some of the German dugouts, however, were far more sophisticated, being three storeys deep with concrete staircases. The recommended British design was to create a series of three parallel trenches linked by the essential communication trenches. The front trench was relatively lightly armed and only usually occupied at the dawn and dusk 'stand to'. The middle trench, referred to as the support trench, provided a retreat for the garrison when the front trench was bombarded. At the rear was the reserve trench, where troops could gather for a counter-attack if the front trenches were taken. Temporary trenches known as 'saps' were also dug, and these usually led from the front trench into no-man's land and were used as a listening post or a position from which to launch a surprise attack.

Over one million men volunteered within the first few months

At the beginning of the war the government had tried to avoid conscription and instead asked for volunteers to join the regular army. They also introduced the concept of the 'Pals' battalions, where men from a town or workplace could join the same battalion. This proved very popular as potential recruits knew they would be working amongst friends and colleagues, so by the beginning of 1915 over a million men had enlisted. The downside of this however was that when Pals battalions were attacked the effect on communities back home could be disastrous, with many of the male population killed or wounded. When 750 members of the Accrington Pals were ordered to attack Serre, nearly 600 were injured or killed in the first twenty minutes of battle. When conscription was introduced in 1916 this system of recruiting was abandoned.

Before being sent to the front all men had to carry out basic training. Officers were brought out of retirement and training camps were soon overflowing as they tried to manage the sudden surge in numbers. Their training was thus very limited and most went to the front totally unprepared for what they were about to do and see. Each battalion sent to the trenches was expected to spend a period of time on the front line, followed by a period in support then a stint in the reserve lines before earning a rest period. The amount of time varied but an average year could be 70 days in the front trenches, 30 in support, 120 in reserve and a precious 70 days resting.

RIGHT: After capturing a German trench near La Boisselle in July 1916, one man from the 11th Battalion, the Cheshire Regiment, keeps watch while his comrades catch some much-needed rest.

Trenches were often three feet deep in water

When trenches were dug in low-lying land they were instantly prone to flooding. Added to this, many of the drainage systems of ditches and water channels originally constructed to drain the area were destroyed by shelling. Armies on the western front were frequently dogged by heavy rain, which could fall for days on end. This combination meant the trenches could be as much as three feet deep in water. Sometimes men would become anchored in the mud and it would take a couple of the other soldiers to dig them out, one foot at a time. Dugouts and cookhouses became flooded, rendering the food inedible. Gumboots were provided but these were often punctured by barbed wire, allowing water to leak through.

ABOVE: Shell-holes became a means of shelter on the Passchendaele battlefield.

Gumboots were provided but these were often punctured by barbed wire, allowing water to leak through.

ABOVE: Canadian troops begin their preparations to go 'over the top' for the assault on the Vimy Ridge during the battle of Arras. They successfully captured 4,000 yards of German-held land.

'Stand to' and the 'morning hate'

It was too dangerous for soldiers to observe the enemy over the top of the trenches as they could be hit by snipers. To avoid this, loopholes were created either by gaps in the sandbags or by the use of trench periscopes. These sometimes consisted simply of two angled mirrors fixed to a long stick, but meant that soldiers could safely watch for enemy movement.

Soldiers were expected to follow a strict routine in the trenches. Each day, an hour before dawn and dusk came 'stand to' (stand to arms), when all men needed to be ready on the fire step with rifles loaded and bayonets fixed. This position would be maintained for up to an hour as they believed most attacks came at this time. 'Stand to' was followed by the 'morning hate', as it came to be known, when infantrymen would fire indiscriminately to relieve the boredom that had set in.

ABOVE AND OPPOSITE:
Soldiers using rudimentary and often camouflaged periscopes spent the daylight hours watching for any movement from the enemy.

Daily chores and daily boredom

'Stand to' was followed by breakfast, brought down in containers from the field kitchens, rifle cleaning and officer inspections. This would include a rigorous scrutiny of weapons and uniforms and often a check for any signs of trench foot. Men would then be given their daily chores, which were normally trench repairs: refilling and repairing sandbags, draining trenches, repairing duckboards and preparing latrines, all carried out below the surface level and out of sight of the enemy. With most of the fighting taking place at night, there was a limit to what could be done during the day, so boredom became a factor, with men limited to reading, writing letters home, playing cards or snatching an extra hour of sleep. 'Stand to' was repeated at dusk and then the trenches became alive. Darkness gave men the opportunity to reach the rear trenches to pick up supplies and water while others took their turn on lookout duty on the fire step. Some would be sent out to patrol no-man's land – often to wait in listening posts to try to glean information from the enemy.

RIGHT: Troops resting outside their dugouts near Bazentin-le-Petit. British troops from the XV Corps had successfully captured the German-held French village.

With most of the fighting taking place at night, there was a limit to what could be done during the day.

ABOVE AND OPPOSITE: Poor weather and low-lying land meant many trenches were flooded, leading to cases of frostbite and trench foot.

Trench foot, trench mouth, trench fever...

At the beginning of the war many men succumbed to trench foot, caused by the constant wet conditions. Blisters and open sores could lead to fungal infections that could make feet swell to two or three times their normal size, with numbness eventually setting in. In severe cases the feet could become gangrenous and this would lead to amputation of the affected parts. Fortunately cases began to decline in 1915 because the army issued troops with extra socks and a greasy ointment, made from whale oil, to protect the skin from the wet conditions. Others succumbed to trench mouth, a painful condition affecting the gums which was caused by a combination of poor oral hygiene, smoking and inadequate nutrition. Added to this was trench fever. Men were constantly plagued by lice in their clothes and delousing was a regular daily routine. In 1918 it was finally discovered that the lice were the cause of trench fever, an illness that caused high temperatures and severe pain. The only cure was to remove men from the trenches, and it would usually take 12 weeks to recover.

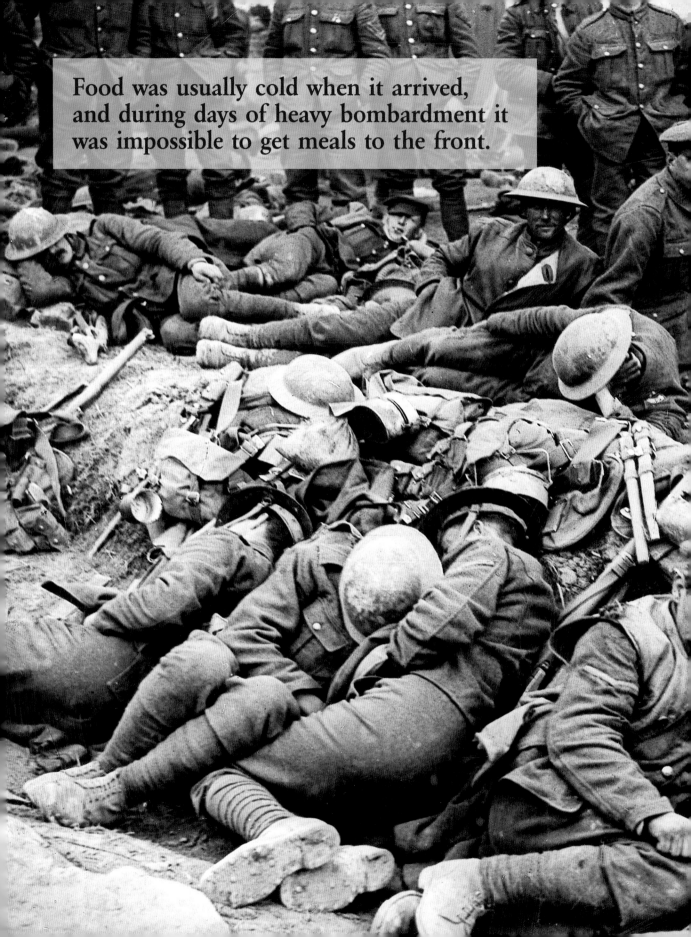

Food was usually cold when it arrived, and during days of heavy bombardment it was impossible to get meals to the front.

Food was often in short supply

The soldiers working on the front line were provided with food by the field kitchen workers. At the start of the war the daily ration was 10 ounces of meat and 8 ounces of vegetables per man, but this was gradually reduced as the army grew larger and German blockades limited the supply. The majority survived on bully beef (canned corned beef), hard biscuits and bread; although with flour soon in short supply the bread was made with dried, ground turnips. Towards the latter part of the war pea soup with a few pieces of horsemeat was the staple food.

Food was cooked in field kitchens, and from there the meals were put into dixies or petrol cans and carried to the trenches in straw-lined boxes. Food was usually cold when it arrived, and during days of heavy bombardment it was impossible to get meals to the front. Some lucky soldiers managed to get hold of primus stoves so they could heat food and brew some tea, although they had to make sure that smoke or steam did not draw attention to the stove.

LEFT: Soldiers constantly craved sleep, so even a muddy bank became a comfortable resting place.

BELOW: A soldier from the Australian Imperial Guard, complete with his own gramophone, listens to music to while away the hours on sentry duty.

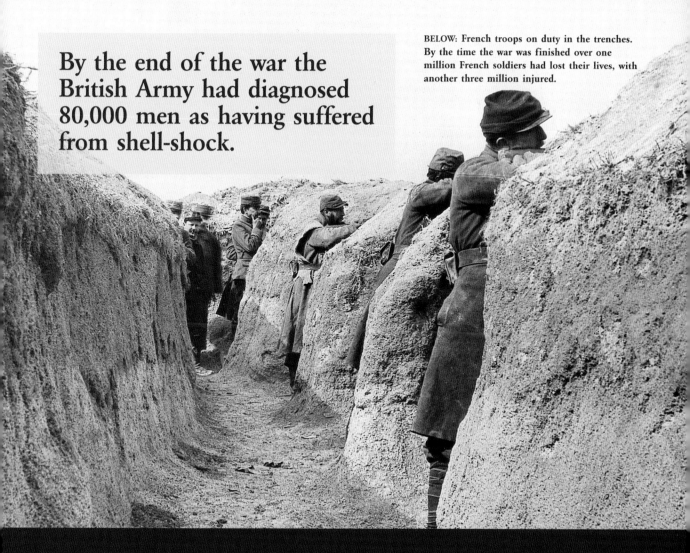

By the end of the war the British Army had diagnosed 80,000 men as having suffered from shell-shock.

BELOW: French troops on duty in the trenches. By the time the war was finished over one million French soldiers had lost their lives, with another three million injured.

Initial symptoms usually led to complete mental breakdown

By the end of the war the British Army had diagnosed 80,000 men as having suffered from shell-shock. Soldiers affected initially suffered from headaches, giddiness, lack of concentration, anxiety and the inability to sleep, but it usually led to a mental breakdown, so they were removed from the front line. At first doctors believed a shell bursting near them had caused injury to the nerves, hence the name. They recommended men were sent home to recover. However, the army was less sympathetic and believed these men were cowards who were shirking their duties, so they were either punished or sent back to the front.

As the war progressed, medical officer Charles Myers began to realise that the trigger was psychological rather than physical, caused by the horrors of war that men had been exposed to. Shell-shock was prevalent among officers, as they were expected to repress any emotion to set an example to their men. As there was so little known about the condition, thousands were still suffering at the end of war and were exposed to a range of experimental treatments. War poet Siegfried Sassoon was a victim of the condition and described its devastating effects in his poem 'Survivors'.

OPPOSITE AND BELOW: British soldiers were first equipped with their familiar bowl-shaped Brodie helmets in 1915, to give them greater protection when they needed to look over the top of the trenches. They were constructed from one piece of steel, which gave the helmet maximum strength.

DAILY MAIL   OCTOBER 17, 1914

Life in the British trenches

Our men have made themselves fairly comfortable in the trenches, in the numerous quarries cut out of the hill-sides, and in the picturesque villages whose steep streets and red-tiled roofs climb the slopes and peep out amid the green and russet of the woods. In the firing line the men sleep and obtain shelter in the dug-outs they have hollowed or 'under-cut' in the sides of the trenches. These refuges are slightly raised above the bottom of the trench, so as to remain dry in wet weather. The floor of the trench is also sloped for purposes of drainage. Some trenches are provided with head cover, the latter, of course, giving protection from the weather as well as from shrapnel balls and splinters of shell.

Considerable ingenuity has been exercised in naming the shelters. Among other favourites are 'The Hotel Cecil', 'The Ritz', 'Hotel Billet-doux', 'Hotel Rue Dormir', etc. On the road barricades, also, are to be found boards bearing the notice: 'This way to the Prussians'.

Obstacles of every kind abound, and at night each side can hear the enemy driving in pickets, for entanglements, digging trous-de-loup, or working forward by sapping. In some places the obstacles constructed by both sides are so close together that some wag has suggested that each should provide working parties to perform this fatiguing duty alternately, since their work is now almost indistinguishable, and serves the same purpose.

The quarries and caves to which allusion has already been made provide ample accommodation for whole battalions, and most comfortable are the shelters which have been constructed in them. The northern slopes of the Aisne Valley are fortunately very steep, and this to a great extent protects us from the enemy's shells, many of which pass harmlessly over our heads to burst in the meadows below, along the river bank. At all points subject to shell fire access to the firing line from behind is provided by communication trenches. These are now so good that it is possible to cross in safety the fire-swept zone to the advanced trenches from the billets in villages, the bivouacs in quarries or the other places where the headquarters of units happen to be.

To those at home the life led by our men and by the inhabitants in this zone would seem strange indeed. All day, and often at night as well, the boom of the guns and the scream of the shells overhead continue. At times, especially in the middle of the day, and after dark, the bombardment slackens; at others it swells into an incessant roar, in which the reports of the different types of gun are merged into one great volume of sound.

There were occasions when ceasefires took place and the most well-known was at Christmas 1914 near Armentieres.

BELOW: On Christmas Eve in 1914 troops emerged from their trenches to meet on the barren no-man's land to exchange greetings and gifts.

OPPOSITE BELOW: A shell-hole near Baumont Hamel was the chosen spot for soldiers to eat their Christmas Day meal in December 1916.

'Not a single shot was fired'

There were occasions when ceasefires took place, and the most well-known was at Christmas 1914 near Armentières. On Christmas Eve opposing troops began singing their own Christmas carols and eventually, after an agreement by officers on both sides, all left the safety of their trenches and met in the middle of no-man's land, exchanged gifts and stories and played football. As the message was shouted from trench to trench, this ceasefire expanded along a 27-mile stretch and continued until the end of Christmas Day, relieving the monotony and the daily challenge of existing in the trenches. In some areas religious ceremonies were held and both sides took the opportunity to recover their respective dead and arrange their burial. The occasional truce took place at Christmas in the years afterwards but these were strongly deterred by officers and therefore very sporadic.

Wound infections often led to gangrene

Soldiers wounded in battle were forced to remain where they fell until it was safe for comrades or stretcher bearers to reach them. Initially they would be taken to the regimental first aid post, which operated at the front line. Those that could not be successfully treated were sent behind the lines to the casualty clearing stations – these would be away from the artillery zone and located where patients could then be transported to hospital if needed.

Despite this chain of medical services the treatments available were still limited and antibiotics were yet to be invented. Shellfire often caused more damage as the debris led to more wound infections, which could potentially become gangrenous. The only cure for this was amputation of the affected part of the body, but this was only partially successful and nearly half of those affected by gangrene subsequently died from their injuries.

ABOVE: A welcome chance to rest at one of the field dressing stations.

OPPOSITE BELOW: Soldiers in the reserve trench waiting for their next orders.

Common infections included typhus, dysentery and cholera. Some also succumbed to exposure as the night-time temperatures frequently fell below freezing.

Thousands died from typhus, dysentry or cholera

As new recruits marched their way to the front line, the first challenge to meet them was the overpowering stench from the trenches. This was caused by a number of factors, including rotting corpses, cordite, the aftermath of poison gas, overflowing cesspits, unwashed bodies, stagnant mud, cigarette smoke and food, and was an indication of what they were about to face. Thousands of men died from infections and the insanitary conditions they were forced to live in. Common infections included typhus, dysentery and cholera. Some also succumbed to exposure as the night-time temperatures frequently fell below freezing.

LEFT: Casualties from the First Battle of Ypres. Although it ended in victory for the Allies, there were significant losses on both sides.

Men closest to the ground were worst affected by gas attacks, and so they inevitably had a greater impact on those who were already injured.

Clouds of yellow-green gas

One of the weapons that troops in the trenches feared most was chlorine gas. The French
initially experimented with tear gas but it did not have any major impact. However, the
Germans began to use chlorine gas during the Second Battle of Ypres in 1915, setting off a
cloud of yellow-green gas that damaged the eyes, nose, throat and lungs of those affected.
It soon became evident that men closest to the ground were worst affected by the toxins,
so gas attacks had a greater impact on those who were already injured. Fortunately the gas
was water-soluble so wet handkerchiefs held over the face would protect personnel. The
British retaliated in the same way but both sides soon realised there was a danger of the wind
blowing the gas back on to their own troops.

The Germans went on to use phosgene and then mustard gas towards the end of the war.
Mustard gas proved to be the most lethal weapon as it was difficult to detect and remained
on the surface of the ground for a long time, lengthening the effects. It could result in nasty
burns that rendered men unfit to fight. By the end of the war gas masks were available to
those working in the trenches, but by the time the Armistice was agreed, it was estimated
that nearly 200,000 British Army personnel had suffered from gas attacks, which continued
to affect men's health long after the war was over.

There was some
development
in wireless
communication
but it was not yet
readily available.

Runners tried to relay messages

A constant issue in the trenches was the inability to communicate and plan methods of attack. There had been some development in wireless communication but it was not yet readily available. Officers therefore relied on homing pigeons, lamps, flares, semaphore, telegraphs and telephones. Soldiers were often used as runners, negotiating the various communication trenches, but as there wasn't a completely reliable method, messages frequently got lost or were so out-of-date when passed on that they became useless. This tended to mean officers had to make instant decisions in the middle of an attack, and the senior commanders had no means of influencing the tactics. On several occasions good opportunities were missed as troops were in the wrong place at the wrong time.

Eight million horses died

An estimated eight million horses died during the war. They were used for cavalry charges at first but it soon became evident that the combination of trenches, barbed wire and machine-gun fire made this very impractical. They were, however, used to transport goods, along with thousands of mules, as they were able to negotiate the rough terrain. It was known that they were good for the troops' morale but manure and their dead carcasses only added to the poor sanitation and risk of disease.

Burying the dead

Neither side was able to bury its dead quickly. Bodies were left in no-man's land and the only time they could be collected was under the cover of darkness: when the front line was moved; or, rarely, when both sides called an unofficial brief truce so the stretcher bearers could go out. By then they were often decomposed and difficult to identify. In some battlefields, burial did not take place until the war was over.

LEFT: Debris and animal carcasses litter the ground after the Battle of Pilckem Ridge in August 1917.

It was a regular night-time task for men to leave the safety of the trenches to repair defences

The average infantryman had four weapons – the rifle, bayonet, shotgun and hand grenade, although the hand grenade became the most useful as it did not need any accuracy or skill and would not expose a man to danger. Battalions also used machine guns and mortars. As the war progressed they were assisted by tanks, which with good tactical planning were able to break through enemy lines more easily.

Barbed wire was heavily used as it was a guaranteed way of slowing an infantryman's movements across the ground, making him an easier target for snipers and machine guns. It was a regular night-time task for men to leave the safety of the trenches and crawl into no-man's land to repair defences.

RIGHT: British infantrymen fixing their bayonets into position as they prepare for attack.

60,000 casualties on the first day alone

Starting in July 1916 and lasting for five months, the Battle of the Somme characterised the full futility of trench warfare. The British Army had 60,000 casualties on the first day alone and this figure rose to 420,000 by the end of the offensive. Added to these figures were half a million Germans and 200,000 French soldiers. Many of these British men were the volunteers from Kitchener's Army - new recruits with only very basic training and with limited equipment - but by the time the battle was eventually called off, the Allies had only gained approximately six miles of ground.

BELOW: German casualties lie in their trench.

By the time the Battle of the Somme was eventually called off the Allies had only gained approximately six miles of ground.

Rats grew to the size of cats

Soldiers were forced to live side by side with millions of rats which gorged themselves on the human remains, some growing to the size of cats. Men frequently tried to kill them with shovels and anything that came to hand, but with one pair of rats producing hundreds of offspring a year, it was a battle they were never going to win. Soldiers often referred to them as corpse-rats. Many believed the rats could sense when heavy bombardment was on the way, as they would suddenly disappear. Added to this, scores of frogs could be found in the waterlogged trenches. Slugs and horned beetles shared their home with the troops, and many men shaved their heads to avoid the invasion of head lice.

ABOVE: Soldiers try to pull an 18-pound field gun out of the mud.

OPPOSITE: One soldier crawls into a dugout in a western Allied trench.

'Over the top' into a 'creeping barrage'

The most common image of World War One fighting strategy was to send thousands of men 'over the top', instructing them to march across no-man's land towards the enemy, leaving them vulnerable to the enemy's hail of bullets. Strategies began to improve as the war progressed, and an advance party was sent ahead to cut through the barbed wire. The artillery fired from behind the trenches just before the attack, but often this had little effect and simply gave the enemy a handy warning. The 'creeping barrage' became more popular where the infantrymen would slowly advance behind a hail of artillery fire and exploding shells. This proved much more successful but the timing needed to be exact.

RIGHT: A line of infantrymen go over the top in Gallipoli. The Dardanelles campaign, a joint venture by the French and British, had attempted to capture Constantinople to create a safe sea route to Russia. The Allies failed in their attempt and over a quarter of a million were injured and 130,000 lost their lives, many from disease in the insanitary conditions.

Stretcher bearers had to flounder through the mud in the dark

Owing to military strategy the wounded generally fell in no-man's land and were forced to wait until the stretcher bearers reached them, waving Red Cross flags in the hope of gaining immunity. The stretcher bearers were often military bandsmen who had been given rudimentary first aid training and were unarmed, which made them easy prey for the enemy. The ground they needed to travel over was often a complete quagmire and it could take as many as six men to carry just one stretcher because of the nature of the terrain. Stretcher bearers, often working in the dark, could easily fall into flooded shell-holes, causing agony for their injured patients, and the journey back to the dressing station could take up to four hours because their progress was so slow.

ABOVE AND OPPOSITE: The stretcher bearers go about their duties in Flanders and return muddy but successful as one injured soldier is rescued.

The ground was often a quagmire and it could take as many as six men to carry just one stretcher.

A barren, soulless swamp

The area between opposite trenches was known as no-man's land. Many new recruits were killed after they ignored instructions not to look over the parapet when their curiosity overcame them. Due to the attritional nature of World War One, the piece of land between the two opposing lines largely remained the same, although the actual width varied between sections from a few hundred yards to over half a mile. Under cover of darkness, troops would be sent across this land to spy on the enemy, recover injured and dead colleagues and repair barbed-wire posts. Due to shelling the land was full of craters which quickly filled with water and turned the ground into soulless swamps with very little sign of vegetation.

RIGHT: Soldiers make their way across a barren stretch of land.

A bolt hole for
protection and shelter

Dugouts, often established within the trench wall, were used as underground shelters and resting places for the troops. Inside there was an opportunity to establish a place to sleep, eat and even socialise if it was large enough, providing cover from shellfire and the elements. Most, supported by wooden posts and protected by corrugated iron, could only house one or two men, but deep dugouts were created for the officers. These had a stairway that could be as much as 10 feet deep, several rooms and often electric light installed. These dugouts gave officers the chance to meet and plan tactics as well as eat and sleep. Many dugouts were protected by gas curtains, which prevented gas from drifting in, but although this offered some protection, there was a danger that a soldier could bring gas in on the soles of his boots, which would affect anyone inside.

ABOVE: The Germans abandoned their trenches after the decision to withdraw to the Hindenburg Line in February 1917.

By the end of the war an estimated 10 million military personnel had lost their lives, with a further 7 million civilians killed.

Over 6,000 miles of trenches were dug

In the last 100 days of the war the Allies successfully began to break through the German trench system. The battle of Amiens began on August 8, 1918, and after a heavy bombardment from the British artillery and the use of 400 tanks, 30,000 German prisoners had been captured in the first four days. Further battles ensued and in September the attack on the Hindenburg Line began, with another 35,000 prisoners captured by the end of the month. The end was now in sight and the Armistice was signed on November 11, 1918, in a railway siding in Compiègne. It came into effect on the eleventh hour of the eleventh day of the eleventh month. The war of attrition was over leaving over 6,000 miles of trenches that were a temporary home to thousands upon thousands of soldiers, snaking their way across the western front.

The Battle of Verdun was the longest of the war, lasting for most of 1916. Over 300,000 men were killed and another 500,000 were wounded.

This is a Transatlantic Press Book
First published in 2012

Transatlantic Press
38 Copthorne Road, Croxley Green, Hertfordshire, UK

© Atlantic Publishing

Photographs © Associated Newspapers Archive

A catalogue record for this book is available from the British Library.

ISBN 978-1-908849-05-2

Printed in China